THE BOOK OF
COMFORT
AND JOY

An *ideals* Publication

Doubleday-Galilee
Doubleday & Company, Inc.,
Garden City, New York 1981

The Lord is my shepherd; I shall not want.

He maketh me to lie down in green pastures; he leadeth me beside the still waters.

He restoreth my soul; he leadeth me in the paths of righteousness for his name's sake.

Yea, though I walk through the valley of the shadow of death, I will fear no evil, for thou art with me; thy rod and thy staff they comfort me.

Thou preparest a table before me in the presence of mine enemies; thou anointest my head with oil; my cup runneth over.

Surely goodness and mercy shall follow me all the days of my life: and I will dwell in the house of the Lord forever.

Psalm 23

ACKNOWLEDGMENTS

BE STRONG by Maltbie Davenport Babcock. From *Thoughts for Everyday Living* (Charles Scribner's Sons, 1901). From *Poems of Inspiration and Courage* by Grace Noll Crowell: "Hope" Copyright 1938 by Harper & Row, Publishers, Inc.; renewed 1966 by Grace Noll Crowell; "Oh, To Live Beautifully" Copyright © 1937 by Harper & Row, Publishers, Inc.; renewed 1968 by Grace Noll Crowell. All Grace Noll Crowell poems reprinted by permission of the publisher. MY HAND IN GOD'S by Florence Scripps Kellogg. From *Daily Word*. Used through courtesy of Unity School of Christianity. WE THANK THEE by William E. Orchard. From *The Treasure Chest*. Reprinted by permission of Harper & Row, Publishers, Inc. By Gertrude M. Puelicher: BUILD YOUR HOUSE UPON THE ROCK; I WILL LIFT UP MINE EYES UNTO THE HILLS; LOVE OF GOD CASTS OUT FEAR; PEACE IS THE SEED THAT CARRIES ITS DIVINITY WITHIN ITSELF. From *God's Corner*, Copyright © 1976 by Gertrude M. Puelicher. All selections had been previously published in *Exclusively Yours*. THIS MORNING by Ann Springsteen. From *It's Me, O Lord* by Anne Springsteen. Concordia Publishing House © 1970. Used by permission. Our sincere thanks to the following authors whose addresses we were unable to locate: Frances Bowles for GOD, KEEP WITHIN MY SOUL...; Louise Driscoll for HOLD FAST YOUR DREAMS; Elma V. Harnetiaux for A WORD TO LIVE BY; Eliza M. Hickok for PRAYER; Joseph Morris for GIVE ME THE COURAGE, LORD.... Verses marked RSV are taken from the Revised Standard Version Bible, copyrighted 1946, 1952, © 1971, 1973. Used by permission. Verses marked TLB are taken from The Living Bible, copyright 1971 by Tyndale House Publishers, Wheaton, Ill. Used by permission.

ISBN: 0-385-17289-3

Library of Congress Catalog Card Number 80-1192

Printed in the United States of America
First Edition

Wait for the Lord; be strong, and let your heart take courage; yea, wait for the Lord!

Psalm 27:14 (RSV)

Give me the courage, Lord, to sail
my boat out from the shore.
I'd rather know the ocean's gale
and hear the tempest's roar
Than anchor safely in some bay
because fear conquered me.
Let craft less daring inland stay . . .
be mine the pathless sea.

Joseph Morris

Courage

When weeping stopped, I saw the earth was green.
I found that hearts can heal and throb again,
That morning's sky is evening's opaline.
When weeping stopped and there was no more pain,
I found that life can sing a glad refrain.

With shoulders straight I scaled the steep ascent,
Crag after crag, forgetful of the force
Below. With shining eyes, I knew content.
My cup is full. My lips can frame a song.
I will go on. I shall be tall and strong.

Mabel Demers Hinckley

A Mighty Fortress Is Our God

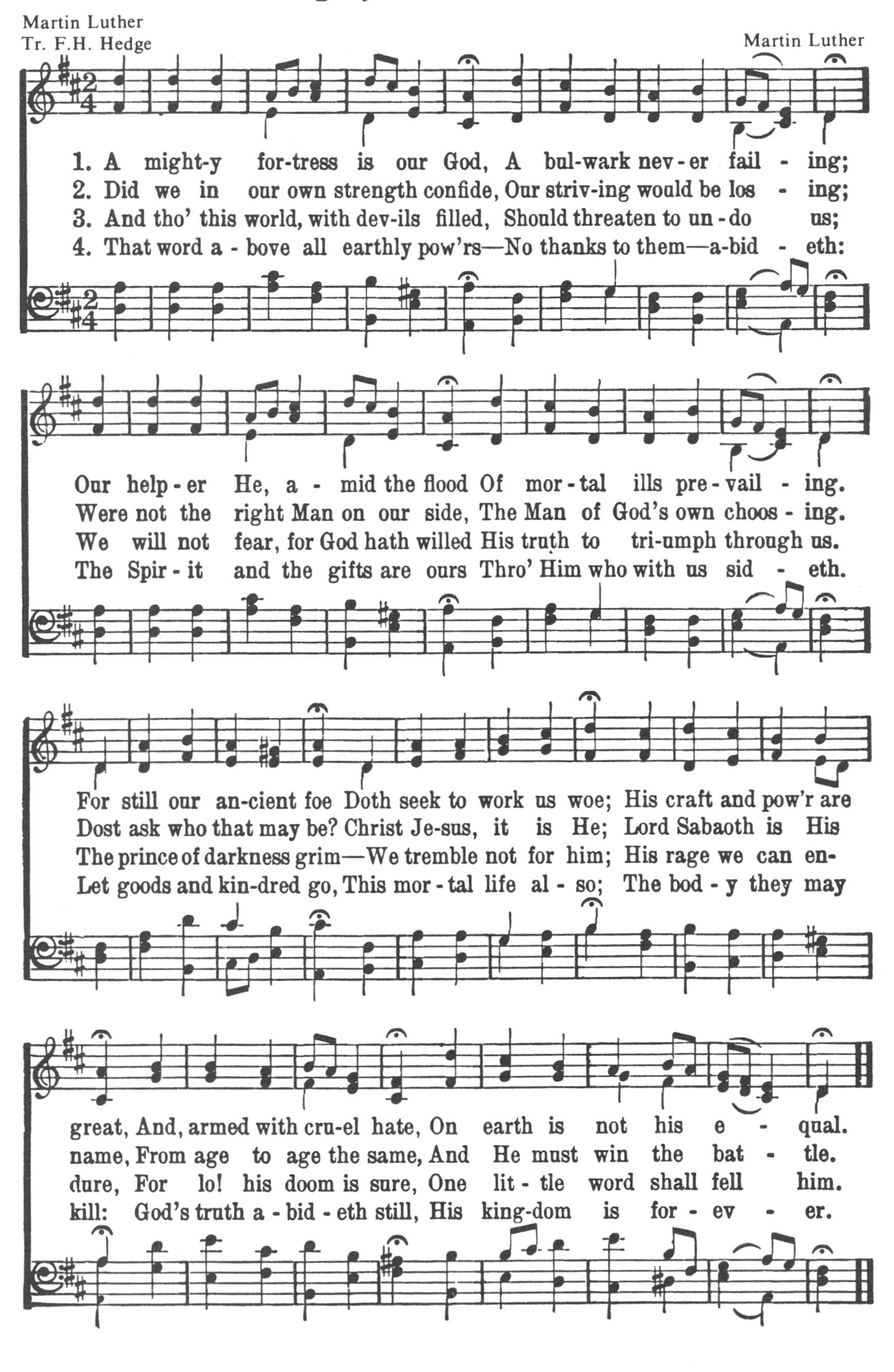
Martin Luther
Tr. F.H. Hedge
Martin Luther
1. A mighty-y for-tress is our God, A bul-wark nev-er fail - ing;
2. Did we in our own strength confide, Our striv-ing would be los - ing;
3. And tho' this world, with dev-ils filled, Should threaten to un-do us;
4. That word a - bove all earthly pow'rs—No thanks to them—a-bid - eth:
Our help-er He, a - mid the flood Of mor-tal ills pre-vail - ing.
Were not the right Man on our side, The Man of God's own choos - ing.
We will not fear, for God hath willed His truth to tri-umph through us.
The Spir-it and the gifts are ours Thro' Him who with us sid - eth.
For still our an-cient foe Doth seek to work us woe; His craft and pow'r are
Dost ask who that may be? Christ Je-sus, it is He; Lord Sabaoth is His
The prince of darkness grim—We tremble not for him; His rage we can en-
Let goods and kin-dred go, This mor-tal life al - so; The bod - y they may
great, And, armed with cru-el hate, On earth is not his e - qual.
name, From age to age the same, And He must win the bat - tle.
dure, For lo! his doom is sure, One lit-tle word shall fell him.
kill: God's truth a - bid - eth still, His king-dom is for - ev - er.

Build your house upon the rock.

I watched a man set a sadistic heel right in the center of a large anthill. He then squatted, Gulliver among the Lilliputians, and chortled scornfully, "Look at these stupid ants. They're running around like crazy with no place to go."

In one sense he was right. Hundreds of ants, confused and bewildered, frightened, I'm sure, at the total destruction of what they had built so carefully, were scurrying frantically in every direction.

How much like ants are we humans! Despite the admonition of the Nazarene Carpenter, we build our houses on the sand, and then when the rains descend, and the floods come, and the winds blow and they all beat against our house until it falls, we run about distractedly, wondering why all this trouble has befallen us.

What does it mean to build one's house on the sand? It means to live one's life apart from that Infinite Invisible that is called God.

The Bible verse "Thou wilt keep him in perfect peace, whose mind is stayed on thee" (Isaiah 26:3) blueprints simply and clearly all we need do if we would find peace. This is a truth upon which we can rely, provided that we comply with the condition imposed, namely, keeping our minds stayed on God.

How does one keep one's mind stayed on God? By being constantly aware of our at-oneness with the Spirit within, by turning to it for advice in every decision we make, for first aid in every emergency. "Man whose breath is in his nostrils" (Isaiah 2:22) is of little account in any situation. There is a vast difference between human variableness and spiritual steadfastness.

Consider for a moment the significance of these six words in Job 32:8: "There is a spirit in man." Say them slowly, ponderingly. You will realize then that we are not merely body with organs that function or fail, with senses that may lose their usefulness. We are far more than we seem to be. There is a Spirit within us, a governing, guiding, directing, maintaining and sustaining divinity that makes straight the way for us—but only when we acknowledge its Presence and its Power.

Then have we followed the Nazarene's advice: we have built our house upon the rock. The rains and floods and winds may come in full force, but our house will not fall. We are rooted and grounded in God, and we are unconquerable.

Gertrude M. Puelicher

Be strong and of good courage; be not frightened, neither be dismayed; for the Lord your God is with you wherever you go.

Joshua 1:9 (RSV)

Be strong!
We are not here to play, to dream, to drift,
We have hard work to do and loads to lift.
Shun not the struggle, face it—'tis God's gift.

Be strong!
Say not the days are evil. Who's to blame?
And fold the hands and acquiesce—O shame!
Stand up, speak out, and bravely, in God's name.

Be strong!
It matters not how deep-entrenched the wrong,
How hard the battle goes, the day how long;
Faint not—fight on! Tomorrow comes the song.

Maltbie Davenport Babcock

Let every dawn of morning be to you as the beginning of life, and every setting sun be to you as its close; then let every one of these short lives leave its sure record of some kindly thing done for others, some goodly strength or knowledge gained for yourself.

John Ruskin

There's One

Sometimes we are forgotten,
Perhaps in hour of need;
But One never forgets us,
Our slightest prayer He'll heed.

Our heavenly Father's moved with
Outpourings of the soul;
He stands ready to help us,
To comfort and console.

Think not that no one hearkens,
Think not that no one cares,
For there is One in glory,
Who every burden shares.

And though you be forgotten
By men of earth, 'tis true,
There's One who never falters . . .
He's there to answer you.

Georgia B. Adams

We Thank Thee

O God, we thank Thee for the world in which thou hast placed us, for the universe whose vastness is revealed in the blue depths of the sky, whose immensities are lit by shining stars beyond the strength of mind to follow. We thank thee for every sacrament of beauty: for the sweetness of flowers, the solemnity of the stars, the sound of streams and swelling seas, for far-reaching lands and mighty mountains which rest and satisfy the soul, the purity of dawn which calls us to holy dedication, the peace of evening which speaks of everlasting rest.

William E. Orchard

Never Give Up

Never give up! There's a rainbow bending
Over the path so dark and steep,
And all of the rain that God is sending
Is for harvests of love you shall some day reap.

Never give up! There's a blessing hidden
Deep in the heart of every woe.
Some happy day it will rise unbidden
As crocus blooms after winter snow.

Never give up! There's a bright star shining
Somewhere in the depths of the darkest night,
And the darkest clouds show their silver lining
When hope returns with the morning light.

Vincent Godfrey Burns

Everlasting Hills

Guarding the valley in great timeless beauty,
Reflecting the glory of God up above,
Mellow with shadows or proud in bright sunshine . . .
We can look to the hills and find strength from His love.

Crested with pink and soft gold of the dawning,
Bold ridges dramatically frame rising sun,
Or washed with a silvery glow by the moonlight,
They whisper night's secrets, mysteriously spun.

Curving and gentle with little homes nestling
In peace on their bosom above the small town,
They beckon hushed fog to follow their contour
Or thrust misty tips into clouds that drift down.

Up from the smoothness of round little hillocks
To Diablo, majestic, with wind in her hair;
Steadfast, invincible, purpled with twilight . . .
One can always find peace and serenity there.

Bird-wakened and freshened, aflutter with promise
On green slopes; wild poppies alerting the spring.
Or drowsing in long golden noon of the summer,
Lazy and sun-baked; tranquillity bring.

Startled aglow by slow fires of bold autumn . . .
Put out every night by twilight's soft haze,
Or brooding and silent and bare through the winter,
Everlasting they stand through years' miniatured days.

Tranquil, quiescent, upsurging, inspiring,
Or gay and alert, fresh-polished with rain;
Fold after fold they encircle the valley . . .
Constantly changing yet always the same.

Nellie Gardner Condon

He Leadeth Me

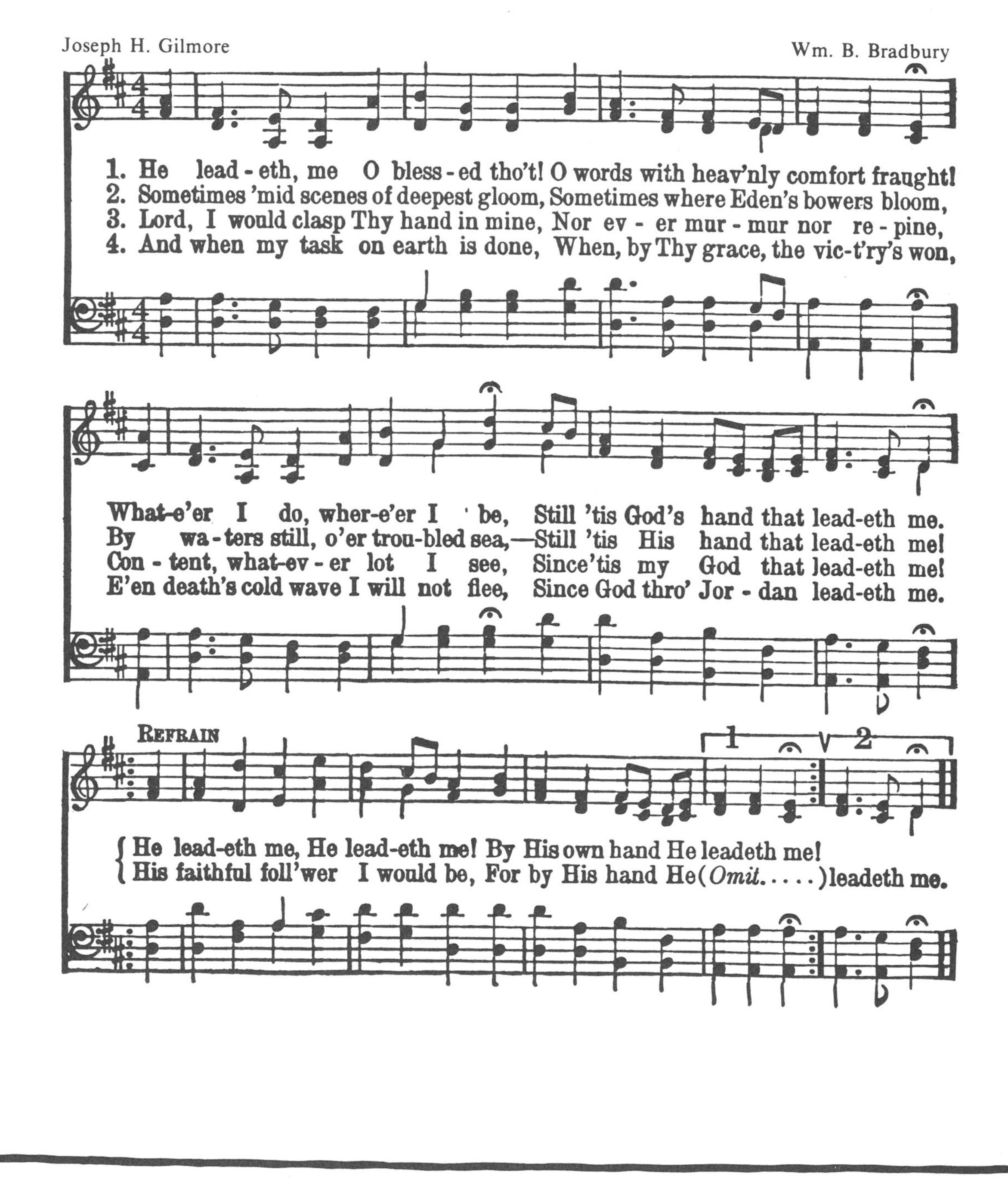

Joseph H. Gilmore
Wm. B. Bradbury
1. He lead - eth, me O bless - ed tho't! O words with heav'nly comfort fraught!
2. Sometimes 'mid scenes of deepest gloom, Sometimes where Eden's bowers bloom,
3. Lord, I would clasp Thy hand in mine, Nor ev - er mur - mur nor re - pine,
4. And when my task on earth is done, When, by Thy grace, the vic-t'ry's won,
What-e'er I do, wher-e'er I be, Still 'tis God's hand that lead-eth me.
By wa - ters still, o'er trou-bled sea,—Still 'tis His hand that lead-eth me!
Con - tent, what-ev - er lot I see, Since 'tis my God that lead-eth me!
E'en death's cold wave I will not flee, Since God thro' Jor - dan lead-eth me.
Refrain
1
2
He lead-eth me, He lead-eth me! By His own hand He leadeth me!
His faithful foll'wer I would be, For by His hand He (Omit. . . . .) leadeth me.

He Leads Me On

O this I know—though shadows deep fall o'er me,
And though the road be rough and dark and long,
My Master walked the selfsame way before me,
And so I journey with a song.
I journey onward with a song!

The winds blow cold, and angry storms assail me,
And heart grows faint, and strength is almost gone;
The sunshine of His love will never fail me,
The night of pain departs with dawn.
The pain departs with glorious dawn!

I see His footprints on the road to glory;
They point the way to glad and great release.
I hear the angels sing the wondrous story;
My heart grows strong and filled with peace.
My soul is filled with His sweet peace!

From the song HE LEADS ME ON, words by June Palmerston, music by Peter Olson.

Trust in the Lord with all your heart,
and do not rely on your own insight.
In all your ways acknowledge him,
and he will make straight your paths.

Proverb 3:5,6 (RSV)

There isn't a tree in the forest,
But God's hand planted it there;
There isn't the smallest wee sparrow,
But He holds it safe in His care.

There isn't a roadway so rugged,
A mountain so high or so steep,
But your God can help you to climb it,
If your hand in His you will keep.

No obstacle lies in your pathway
To keep you from reaching your goal,
But God can help you to surmount it,
If He is in charge of your soul.

So trust in your Heavenly Father,
Take heart in His love, His calm,
For He will take care of His children;
He holds their whole world in His palm.

Vera Baisel

It is not the quantity of thy faith that shall save thee; a drop of water is as true water as the whole ocean.

Rev. J. Welsh

Lord, increase our faith. We believe; help Thou our unbelief. Give us a true child's trust in Thee in all thy strength and goodness. Cause us to rest with perfect confidence in all thy purposes and ways. Enable us to confide all our interests for time and for eternity to thy keeping. Give us, heavenly Father, the substance of things hoped for and the evidence of things unseen, that we may walk by faith, not by sight, looking not at the things which are seen and temporal but at those things which are not seen and eternal.

Author Unknown

Give me a humble spirit, Lord,
Where wisdom will take root
And help me then to cultivate
Each tender, budding shoot;

Endow me with a thirst for truth,
Deny me self-content,
And make me useful in this world
Until my life is spent.

Give me a faith that's strong
and sure
Above all temporal things,
Give me a sense of humor to
Offset life's tiresome stings.

And finally, Lord, make me sincere
In all I do and say
That I may build an inner fort
Which nothing can dismay.

Viney Wilder

I do not ask that every dawn be radiant ...Or constant sunshine fall across my way...But only that despite the clouds o'erspreading my faith may make today a sun-filled day . . . I do not ask great joy at every turning...Upon the path my feet have learned to tread... But only that I recognize the gladness that love today about my steps has spread...I do not ask that sometime I may enter some far-off Heaven whose countless ages roll...But only that in finding truth illumined I gain a Heaven today within my soul.

Betsey Buttles

Our sincere thanks to the author
whose address we were unable to locate.

My Faith Looks Up to Thee

Ray Palmer
Lowell Mason
1. My faith looks up to Thee, Thou Lamb of Cal - va - ry,
2. May Thy rich grace im-part Strength to my faint - ing heart,
3. While life's dark maze I tread, And griefs a - round me spread,
4. When ends life's tran - sient dream, When death's cold, sul - len stream
Sav - iour di - vine! Now hear me while I pray; Take all my
My zeal in - spire. As Thou hast died for me, Oh, may my
Be Thou my Guide. Bid dark - ness turn to day; Wipe sor - row's
Shall o'er me roll, Blest Sav - iour, then in love Fear and dis -
guilt a - way. Oh, let me from this day Be whol - ly Thine!
love to Thee Pure, warm, and change-less be, A liv - ing fire!
tears a - way; Nor let me ev - er stray From Thee a - side!
trust re - move. Oh, bear me safe a - bove, A ran - somed soul!

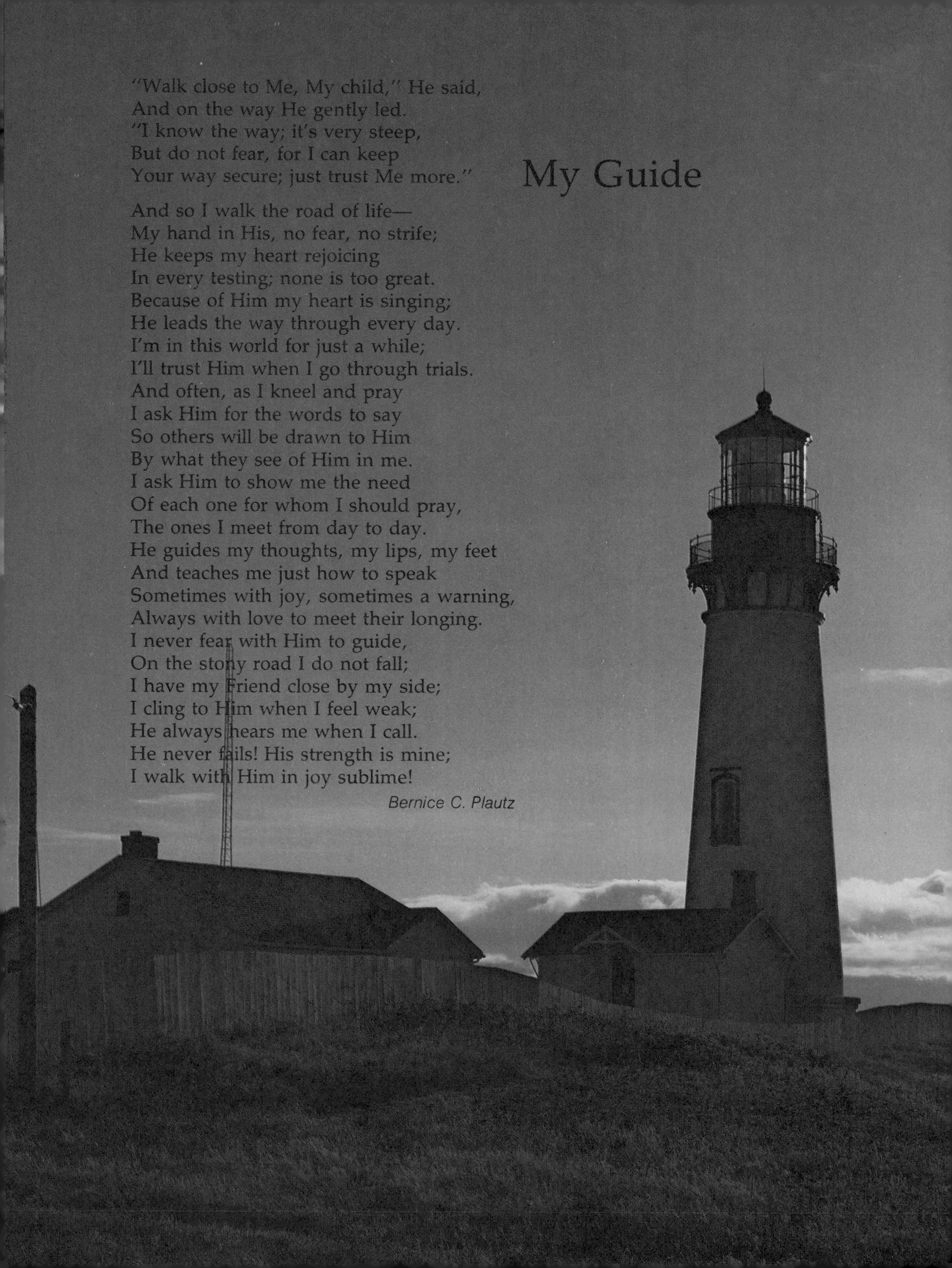

My Guide

"Walk close to Me, My child," He said,
And on the way He gently led.
"I know the way; it's very steep,
But do not fear, for I can keep
Your way secure; just trust Me more."

And so I walk the road of life—
My hand in His, no fear, no strife;
He keeps my heart rejoicing
In every testing; none is too great.
Because of Him my heart is singing;
He leads the way through every day.
I'm in this world for just a while;
I'll trust Him when I go through trials.
And often, as I kneel and pray
I ask Him for the words to say
So others will be drawn to Him
By what they see of Him in me.
I ask Him to show me the need
Of each one for whom I should pray,
The ones I meet from day to day.
He guides my thoughts, my lips, my feet
And teaches me just how to speak
Sometimes with joy, sometimes a warning,
Always with love to meet their longing.
I never fear with Him to guide,
On the stony road I do not fall;
I have my Friend close by my side;
I cling to Him when I feel weak;
He always hears me when I call.
He never fails! His strength is mine;
I walk with Him in joy sublime!

Bernice C. Plautz

My Hand in God's

Each morning when I wake I say,
"I place my hand in God's today."
I know He'll walk close by my side,
My every wandering step to guide.

He leads me with the tenderest care
When paths are dark and I despair.
No need for me to understand,
If I but hold fast to His hand.

My hand in His! No surer way
To walk in safety through each day.
By His great bounty I am fed,
Warmed by His love, and comforted.

When at day's end I seek my rest
And realize how much I'm blessed,
My thanks pour out to Him; and then
I place my hand in God's again.

Florence Scripps Kellogg

I Have Faith

I have faith in the new day that's coming,
  In the things that I know I shall do;
I have faith that there'll be something
  lovely for me.
And I've faith in myself, have you?

I believe that our God will watch over,
  And I know that He'll always take care;
And if things go wrong, we shall still
  have a song
And a happiness always to share.

That's why I have faith in tomorrow,
  Though today might be lonely and blue;
My best I shall give, in each new day I live,
  And my own faith will carry me through.

Garnett Ann Schultz

Almighty God, Lord of the storm and of the calm, the vexed sea and the quiet haven, of day and night, of life and of death; grant unto us so to have our hearts stayed upon they faithfulness, thine unchangingness and love, that whatsoever betide us, however black the cloud or dark the night, with quiet faith trusting in Thee, we may look upon Thee with untroubled eye, and walking in lowliness towards Thee, and in lovingness towards one another, abide all storms and troubles of this mortal life, beseeching Thee that they may turn to the soul's true good; we ask it for thy mercy's sake.

George Dawson

Therefore he will listen to me
and answer when I call to him.

Psalm 4:3 (TLB)

I know not by what methods rare,
But this I know—God answers prayer.
I know that He has given His word
Which tells me prayer is always heard,
And will be answered, soon or late,
And so I pray and calmly wait.

I know not if the blessing sought
Will come in just the way I thought,
But leave my prayers with Him alone,
Whose will is wiser than my own,
Assured that He will grant my quest,
Or send some answer far more blest.

Eliza M. Hickok

This Morning

Life has begun again, Father.

You have given me another day of grace,
another day to live;
  to speak to someone,
  to touch someone,
  to ask for something,
  to take something,
  to give something.

Whatever I make of this day,
whatever I become this day
I put into Your hands.

Anne Springsteen

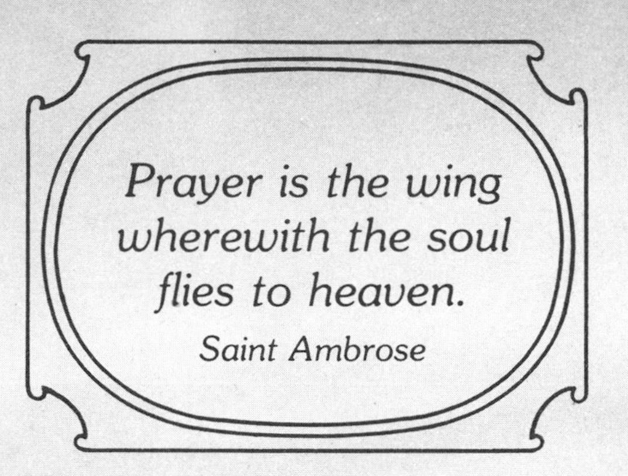
Prayer is the wing
wherewith the soul
flies to heaven.
Saint Ambrose

A Morning Prayer

The day returns
and brings us the petty round
of irritating concerns and duties.
Help us to play the man,
help us to perform them
with laughter and kind faces,
let cheerfulness abound with industry.
Give us to go blithely
on our business all this day,
bring us to our resting beds
weary and content and undishonored,
and grant us in the end
the gift of sleep.

Robert Louis Stevenson

Sweet Hour of Prayer

W.W. Walford

Wm. B. Bradbury

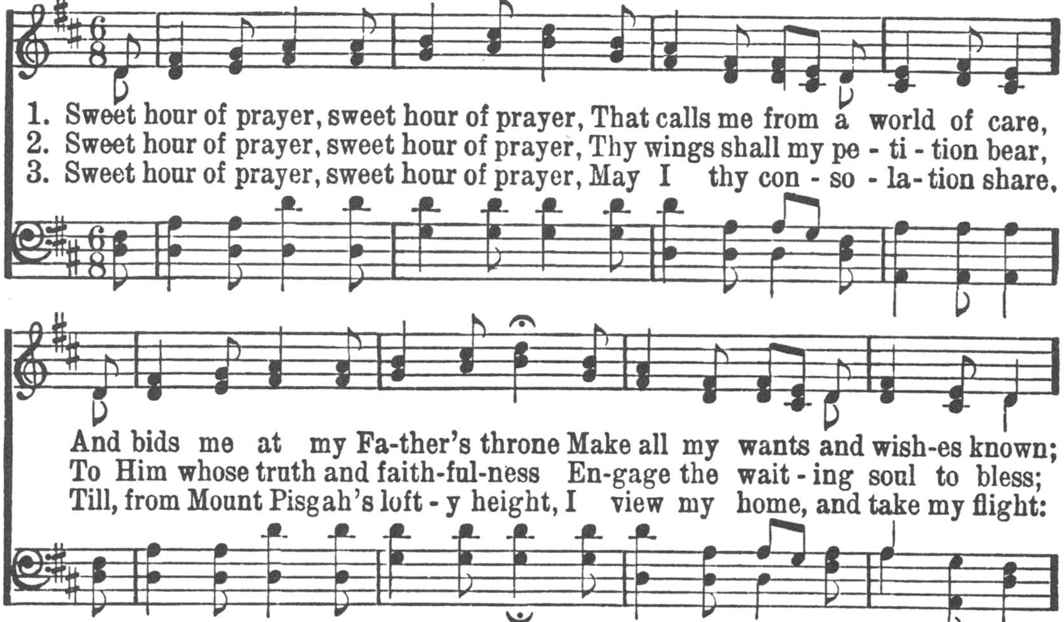

1. Sweet hour of prayer, sweet hour of prayer, That calls me from a world of care,
2. Sweet hour of prayer, sweet hour of prayer, Thy wings shall my pe - ti - tion bear,
3. Sweet hour of prayer, sweet hour of prayer, May I thy con - so - la- tion share,

And bids me at my Fa-ther's throne Make all my wants and wish-es known;
To Him whose truth and faith-ful-ness En-gage the wait - ing soul to bless;
Till, from Mount Pisgah's loft - y height, I view my home, and take my flight:

In sea - sons of dis - tress and grief, My soul has oft - en found re - lief,
And since He bids me seek His face, Be-lieve His word and trust His grace,
This robe of flesh I'll drop, and rise To seize the ev - er - last - ing prize;

And oft es-caped the tempter's snare, By thy re - turn, sweet hour of prayer.
I'll cast on Him my ev - 'ry care, And wait for thee, sweet hour of prayer.
And shout, while passing thro' the air, Farewell, fare-well, sweet hour of prayer!

This Moment

I may never see tomorrow; there's no written guarantee,
And things that happened yesterday belong to history.
I cannot predict the future, and I cannot change the past.
I have just the present moment; I must treat it as my last.

I must use this moment wisely for it soon will pass away,
And be lost to me forever as a part of yesterday.
I must exercise compassion, help the fallen to their feet,
Be a friend unto the friendless, make an empty life complete.

I must make this moment precious for it will not come again,
And I can never be content with things that might have been.
Kind words I fail to say this day may ever be unsaid,
For I know not how short may be the path that lies ahead.

The unkind things I do today may never be undone,
And friendships that I fail to win may nevermore be won.
I may not have another chance on bended knee to pray,
And thank my God with humble heart for giving me this day.

I may never see tomorrow, but this moment is my own.
It's mine to use or cast aside; the choice is mine, alone.
I have just this precious moment in the sunlight of today,
Where the dawning of tomorrow meets the dusk of yesterday.

Paul F. Barnett

In an Old Church

The faded frescoes do not touch my heart
Nor ancient altarpiece nor rood nor choir,
With reverence translated into art.
Each soaring column, vaulted arch and spire
Awakens admiration, but I feel
Less moved by them than lighted candles' glow
And stone worn deeply where the people kneel
As ceaseless generations come and go.

Nine hundred years of prayer encircle me,
With deepest aspirations, joy and grief.
The song of faith resounds exultantly
To tell the age-old triumph of belief.
Encompassed by an unseen host today,
My pilgrim soul now pauses here to pray.

Gail Brook Burket

meditation

Lord, help me find in every day
A moment when my soul can pray...
Whether it be at early morn
Or in the silvery light of moon...
To keep my mind from evil thought,
To keep my heart from evil wrought,
To give me courage, strength anew
To teach me thine own works to do:
To cleanse the inner life of me
To make me what I ought to be,
That I may grow in faith and power,
Lord, hear me in the quiet hour.

Grace Mathews Walker

God, silence my voice
Until thy spirit within me
Makes union with Thee
That I may utter words
Of truth, wisdom, beauty, peace.
If this should be,
Words neither hurt nor bruise.
They become divine instruments
In communication with my fellows.

Myrtle Beeler Day

Thanks, Eternal One, for occasional moments of quietness . . . Moments when there is such serenity of soul that noises go unheard... And distractions do not distract... Moments of calm growing into minutes of joy, when we can be in harmony with our fellowman, and at one with Thee... May such times come often for all of us. Amen.

Samuel F. Pugh

Make me like a deep, quiet pool, God,
With a surface unruffled, serene,
So the beauty above and around me
Is mirrored, clear-cut and clean.

Make me like the cool desert waters,
Giving those with a thirst-
driven stride,
Needed strength and life-giving power
To go on refreshed, satisfied.

Make me like a clear
mountain brook, God,
Shouting a song as I run
Each spray that is dashed off
the jagged rocks,
A sparkling gem in the sun.

Edna B. Stark

What A Friend

Joseph Scriven
Charles Converse
1. What a Friend we have in Je - sus, All our sins and griefs to bear!
2. Have we tri - als and temp - ta - tions? Is there troub-le an - y - where?
3. Are we weak and heav-y - la - den, Cumbered with a load of care?—
What a priv - i - lege to car - ry Ev - 'ry-thing to God in prayer!
We should nev-er be dis - cour-aged, Take it to the Lord in prayer.
Pre - cious Sav-ior, still our ref - uge,—Take it to the Lord in prayer.
O what peace we oft - en for - feit, O what need-less pain we bear,
Can we find a friend so faith - ful Who will all our sor-rows share?
Do thy friends despise, for-sake thee? Take it to the Lord in prayer;
All be-cause we do not car - ry Ev - 'ry-thing to God in prayer!
Je - sus knows our ev - 'ry weak - ness, Take it to the Lord in prayer.
In His arms He'll take and shield thee, Thou wilt find a sol - ace there.

Hope in God! I shall yet praise him again.
Yes, I shall again praise him for his help.

Psalm 42:5 (TLB)

Hope is a word to live by.

Hope is something within us that makes us strive and reach for something higher.

There may be failure, but there is always hope to start again, with hope directing our way.

Hope longs for a desired goal.

Hope keeps us with a song in our hearts.

Hope is a booster for the discouraged.

Hope is a stepping-stone to the depressed and needy; it renews their will to find a brighter day.

Hope is confidence and expectation.

Hope is a guide to good cheer and happiness.

Hope is a comfort when fear assails us.

Hope brings light into darkness.

Hope is truly a word to live by.

Elma V. Harnetiaux

HOPE

This would I hold more precious than fine gold,
This would I keep although all else be lost:
Hope in the heart, that precious, priceless thing,
Hope at any cost.

And God, if its fine luster should be dimmed,
If seemingly through grief it may be spent,
Help me to wait without too much despair—
Too great astonishment.

Let me be patient when my spirit lacks
Its high exuberance, its shining wealth;
Hope is a matter often, God, I know,
Of strength…of health.

Help me to wait until the strength returns;
Help me to climb each difficult high slope;
Always within my heart some golden gleam—
Some quenchless spark of hope.

Grace Noll Crowell

"I will lift up mine eyes unto the hills"

Regardless of one's interpretation of the Bible, some of its verses bring comfort, particularly in times of duress. One such verse is Psalm 121:1, "I will lift up mine eyes unto the hills, from whence cometh my help." We have no need to move out of our chairs to do this. We need merely close our eyes for a second and let our thoughts lift themselves. You may hesitate to believe that this is a possibility, but take my word for it. Just sit comfortably in your chair, close your eyes and relax in those words, "I will lift up mine eyes unto the hills, from whence cometh my help." Almost immediately you will find yourself being flooded with peace—peace that comes from within yourself, comforting serenity that can mean only one thing—God is on the field, God is taking over.

Gradually you will gain a sense of not needing to struggle with a problem or battle with a neighbor or compete with an associate. You will find yourself resting in the security of God's presence, and if you take time for it, you will be able to feel that presence.

We have grown so accustomed to pushing buttons in this mechanical age that there are those who expect they can push a button and presto, chango, there is God-power or God-presence operating in their behalf.

What a blessing it is that no paternalistic government can legislate God for us! Anti-poverty programs may be legislated; federal aid may be legislated; even war may be legislated. All this legislation humanly planned may just as quickly and humanly be rescinded by legislation, but not God. God is completely immune from legislation of any kind, and just as "before Abraham was, I am," so will it be unto eternity.

The Creative Principle of the universe is untouchable by man or man-made laws simply because God is law. As a result, all attempts to explain God are completely individual. No matter how regularly we attend church, no matter how devoted we may be to church projects, no matter how many books we read on metaphysics, the fact remains that we ourselves are the only ones who can reach the Father within us.

Jesus the Christ proved His own words, "The Father that dwelleth in me, he doeth the works" (John 14:10). And as we reach the Father within us, we can live as Jesus did in that same God-presence. It will govern our lives, showing us where to go and what to do, if we do our part by taking time each day to practice it. Practicing the presence of God has its beginning in lifting our "eyes unto the hills, from whence cometh our help."

Gertrude M. Puelicher

Because I Have Seen the Mountains

Because I have seen the mountains,
  Because I have looked so long
Where the peaks rise on the far skies,
  And heard the sea's song—

My soul is eager for climbing,
  My spirit's wings are strong,
Because I have strayed where the hills prayed,
  And heard the sea's song.

Anne Campbell

Belief

I do not always understand
The many things I see:
The hills that climb to meet the sky,
The shore that finds the sea,
A shining star at close of day
As twilight gathers near,
And then the darkness all about
As night is quickly here.

I do not always analyze
The things before my eyes:
The mysteries too deep to know,
The hours of sweet surprise,
A stream that flows through valleys deep,
The river rushing on,
The desert sand so dry and still,
The day that's here and gone.

Belief is mine; although 'tis true
I know not how or why,
The rain shall end as it began
And sunshine light the sky.
'Tis faith alone that tells my heart
The winter too shall pass,
And spring will come to bless the world
An April day at last.

I cannot always understand
These miracles of God;
But one day all of us shall walk
The path that angels trod.
Still, I believe and always shall
In so much yet unseen;
Because a faith lives in my heart,
Belief is mine supreme.

Garnett Ann Schultz

Sun on Stone

Hope is like the sun upon the threshold of the heart. A glow lights up the inner room. The shadows fall apart, and rising to unlatch the door we cast all fear away as we venture out into the brightness of the day.

Hope is like a ray of sunlight falling on gray stone. The heart is warmed. We're tempted out to take the road alone, out towards a broad horizon where the sky is gold with promise of the love of God and blessings manifold.

Patience Strong

Hope

Hope is a robin singing
On a rainy day;
He knows the sun will shine again
Though skies may now be gray.

Like the robin let us be,
Meet trouble with a smile;
And soon the sun will shine for us
In just a little while.

Beverly J. Anderson

Hope is a looking forward to something with an earnest belief. Often it means an expectancy of light when one is still in darkness. I like to think of it as the promise of dawn to follow the night shadows. Life takes new strength and meaning where there is hope. Let us keep this promise in our hearts.

Esther Baldwin York

What is impossible with men is possible with God.

Luke 18:27

I live on hopes and I live on
dreams;
At times I thrive on impossibilities
it seems,
But are you the one to tell me I'm
wrong
Or will you share my dreams and
come along?

There really is nothing that is
impossible it seems
If you really believe and work
endlessly toward these dreams.
Of course, you realize, you must be
realistic along the way;

For all dreams and no reality is
merely child's play.
And reality is a big part of
dreaming, too,
For it's the blending of both that
makes those dreams come true.

Mary Jane Cook

Greatness

A man is as great as the dreams he dreams,
As great as the love he bears,
As great as the values he redeems,
As the happiness he shares.

A man is as great as the thoughts he thinks,
As the worth he has attained,
As the fountains at which his spirit drinks,
As the insight he has gained.

A man is as great as the truth he speaks,
As great as the help he gives,
As great as the destiny he seeks,
As great as the life he lives.

Author Unknown

Once More Tall

When I behold the heavens, Lord,
The sun and moon and stars,
And think upon the worlds that lie
Beyond the planet Mars,
I shrink into my smallest self,
Even smaller than a mote,
And wonder God should take of me
The very slightest note.
Then I see sparrows in the wind
And know God marks their fall;
My soul swells up with God's great love,
And I am once more tall.

Minnie Klemme

Hold Fast Your Dreams

Louise Driscoll

Hold fast your dreams!
Within your heart
Keep one still, secret spot
Where dreams may go,
And, sheltered so,
May thrive and grow
Where doubt and fear are not.

O keep a place apart,
Within your heart,
For little dreams to go!

Think still of lovely things that are not true.
Let wish and magic work at will in you.
Be sometimes blind to sorrow. Make believe!
Forget the calm that lies
In disillusioned eyes.
Though we all know that we must die,
Yet you and I
May walk like gods and be
Even now at home in immortality.
We see so many ugly things—
Deceits and wrongs and quarrelings;
We know, alas! we know
How quickly fade
The color in the west,
The bloom upon the flower,
The bloom upon the breast
And youth's blind hour.
Yet keep within your heart
A place apart
Where little dreams may go,
May thrive and grow.
Hold fast—hold fast your dreams!

Endymion

A thing of beauty is a joy forever:
Its loveliness increases; it will never
Pass into nothingness; but still will keep
A bower quiet for us, and a sleep
Full of sweet dreams, and health, and quiet breathing.
Therefore, on every morrow, are we wreathing
A flowery band to bind us to the earth,
Spite of despondence, of the inhuman dearth
Of noble natures, of the gloomy days,
Of all the unhealthy and o'er-darkened ways
Made for our searching: yes, in spite of all,
Some shape of beauty moves away the pall
From our dark spirits. Such the sun, the moon,
Trees old, and young, sprouting a shady boon
For simple sheep; and such are daffodils
With the green world they live in; and clear rills
That for themselves a cooling covert make
'Gainst the hot season; the mid-forest brake,
Rich with a sprinkling of fair musk-rose blooms:
And such too is the grandeur of the dooms
We have imagined for the mighty dead;
All lovely tales that we have heard or read:
An endless fountain of immortal drink,
Pouring unto us from the heaven's brink.

Nor do we merely feel these essences
For one short hour; no, even as the trees
That whisper round a temple become soon
Dear as the temple's self, so does the moon,
The passion poesy, glories infinite,
Haunt us till they become a cheering light
Unto our souls, and bound to us so fast,
That, whether there be shine, or gloom o'ercast,
They always must be with us, or we die.

John Keats

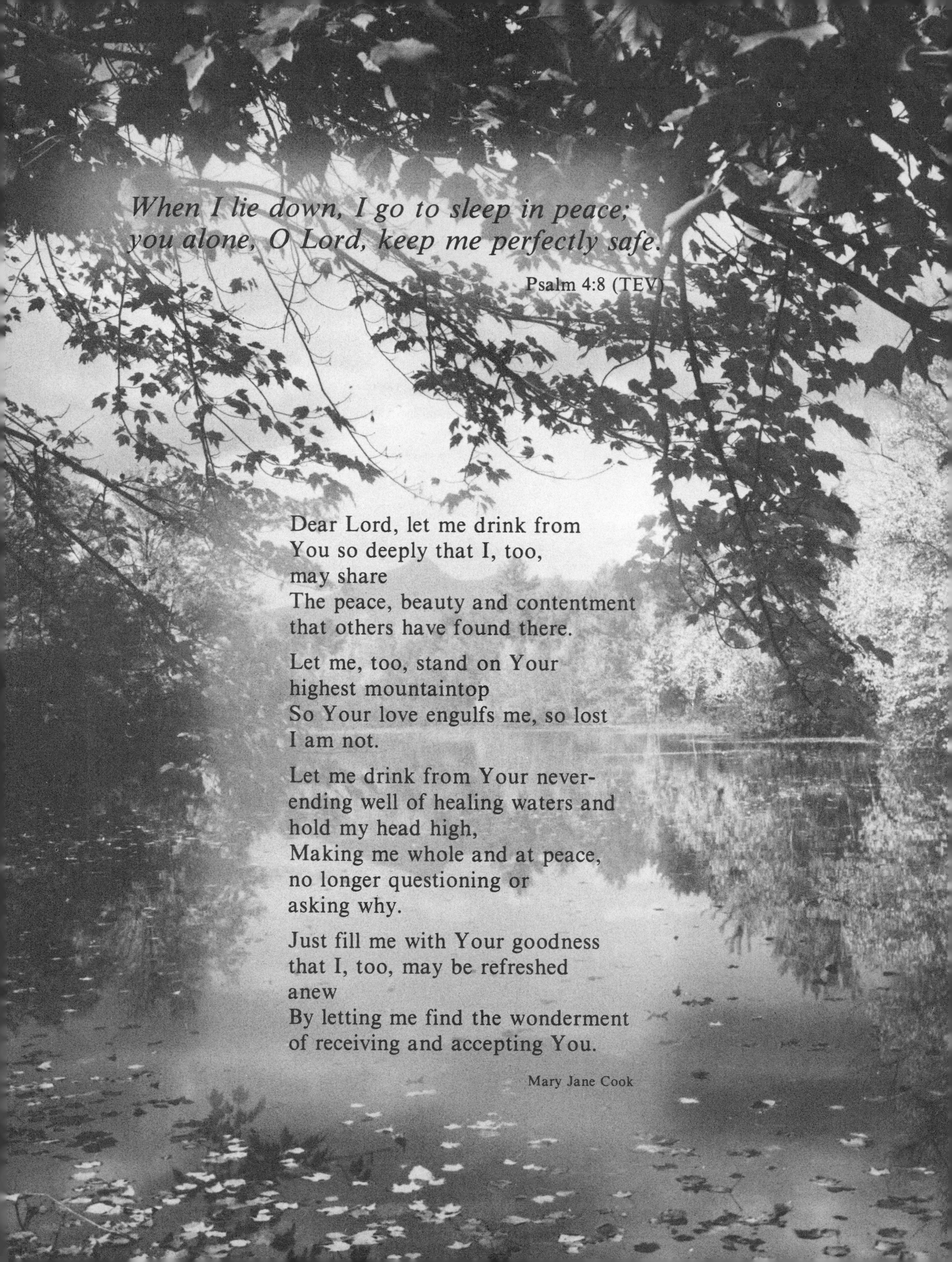

When I lie down, I go to sleep in peace;
you alone, O Lord, keep me perfectly safe.

Psalm 4:8 (TEV)

Dear Lord, let me drink from
You so deeply that I, too,
may share
The peace, beauty and contentment
that others have found there.

Let me, too, stand on Your
highest mountaintop
So Your love engulfs me, so lost
I am not.

Let me drink from Your never-
ending well of healing waters and
hold my head high,
Making me whole and at peace,
no longer questioning or
asking why.

Just fill me with Your goodness
that I, too, may be refreshed
anew
By letting me find the wonderment
of receiving and accepting You.

Mary Jane Cook

Peace is the seed that carries its divinity within itself.

Have you ever planted a seed in a pot or in a garden and then watered and tended it as it slowly took root? Tiny green shoots finally appear, and develop eventually into a full-grown plant. The life force in that seed sent it on its way to fulfill its purpose.

A man has once again dropped the seed of peace into the consciousness of the peoples of the world. He is not a teacher or master who has been sent on a divine mission. He is an ordinary being, such as you and I. Yet he has had the courage to drop that word peace into human consciousness. His sincerity seems genuine. His desire, apparently, is to achieve peace for this country as well as for the world. The question is, who will nurture this seed of peace he is trying to sow? Who will tend it faithfully until it is firmly rooted in the consciousness of each of us, in world consciousness?

Nearly 2000 years ago there came a Man whose mission was prearranged. It bore the stamp of divinity. He too tried to sow the seed of peace—He called it "my peace." He said, "Peace I leave with you, my peace give I unto you: not as the world giveth, give I unto you" (John 14:27). Later, that seed came to be known as Christianity, with love and peace its component parts, love for God and man, and peace for all nations.

Unfortunately, love and peace sank almost into oblivion, leaving Christianity to limp along as best it could. Criticism, condemnation, prejudice, suspicion, intolerance, jealousy—whether these appear in business, politics, neighborhoods, or among members of a family, they ring the death knell to peace. These are the barriers that result in bitterness, resentment and eventual separation into factions. These are the forerunners of war, the tares that must be uprooted if we would find "my peace."

Peace is the seed that carries its divinity within itself. All it needs for growth is the acceptance and nourishment that you and I can give. It can be sent winging its way around the universe provided that you and I become aware of the importance of maintaining peace in our daily experience. That involves overlooking the little idiosyncrasies and eccentricities of those with whom we come into daily contact just as we hope they will overlook ours. That involves, not a smug tolerance, a so-called Christian forbearing; that involves kindly understanding, a desire and effort to live at peace with everyone. War is a characteristic of humanhood motivated by fear, greed, hate, politics, or a determination to subdue and dominate.

It exists only on the human plane. Peace exists only on the spiritual plane; its motivation is divine—love for God and for one's fellowman, whether he be your next-door neighbor or your neighbor across the world. War with its horrors, heartbreaks and tragedies will be eliminated only as you and I strive hourly for "the peace of God which passeth all understanding" (Philippians 4:7); as we root that peace so firmly in our consciousness that each of us will pray as fervently as did St. Francis of Assisi when he said, "Lord, make me an instrument of thy peace." We are told that the "prayer of a righteous man availeth much" (James 5:16). What then is hindering us?

Gertrude M. Puelicher

The swaying trees sigh contentment to the sky;
Ceaseless flow of murmuring water soothes
The harried heart and hurried feet; soft music . . .
Song of the wild, peace for my soul . . .
This I find . . .
at the bend of the river.

Arthur J. Weber

Peace

Peace is looking at a child
With eyelids closed in sleep
And knowing that the love of God
Is constant, true and deep.

Peace is gazing into depths
Of water, cool and clear,
And knowing fast within your heart
That God is ever near.

Peace is hearing birds that sing
In harmony of voice,
And knowing that you, too, can live
With God's own way your choice.

Peace is living day by day
With His own company,
So you will have within your soul
Divine tranquility.

Mildred Spires Jacobs

Purpose

Dear Lord, may others find in me
A pool of cool tranquility;
A quiet resting place to find
New strength of heart and peace of mind.

May all who stop within my gate
Find solace here; exchange the hate
For love that ever-widening dwells
Outside the circle of themselves.

And may I have the listening ear
That helps dispel all doubt and fear.
In days of dark uncertainty,
Lord, place an inner light in me.

Lord, should my inner light be low,
Help Thy unfailing grace to grow,
That all who come to me with care
May see Thy love reflected there.

Margaret Freer

It Is Well With My Soul

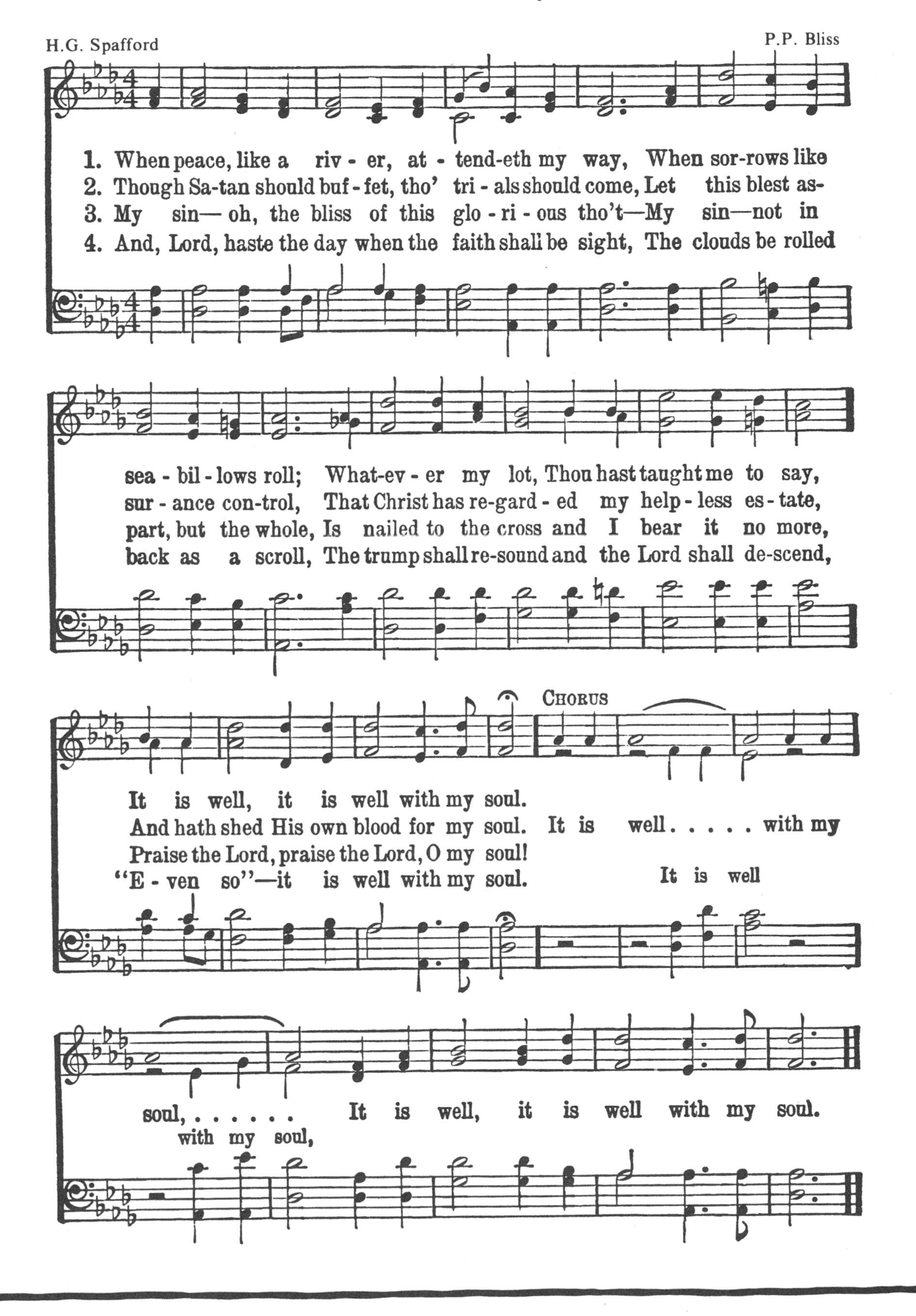
H.G. Spafford
P.P. Bliss
1. When peace, like a riv - er, at - tend-eth my way, When sor-rows like
2. Though Sa-tan should buf - fet, tho' tri - als should come, Let this blest as-
3. My sin— oh, the bliss of this glo - ri - ous tho't—My sin—not in
4. And, Lord, haste the day when the faith shall be sight, The clouds be rolled
sea - bil - lows roll; What-ev - er my lot, Thou hast taught me to say,
sur - ance con-trol, That Christ has re-gard - ed my help - less es - tate,
part, but the whole, Is nailed to the cross and I bear it no more,
back as a scroll, The trump shall re-sound and the Lord shall de-scend,
CHORUS
It is well, it is well with my soul.
And hath shed His own blood for my soul. It is well. . . . . with my
Praise the Lord, praise the Lord, O my soul!
"E - ven so"—it is well with my soul.
It is well
soul, ... It is well, it is well with my soul.
with my soul,

Woodland Communion

There's a deep sweet peace
Enters in my soul
As I walk through the Shadowed Woodland
And I lift my hands
And my heart to God
In a wordless prayer of joy.
It is here I can feel His hand in mine;
Here, in this mystic stillness
I can hear His voice
In the whispering leaves
Full of love and sweet compassion
Saying "Child of mine, take heart, have
Faith, for I am with you always."
My being thrills with ecstasy
In the fullness of His Presence,
And I go again to the daily tasks
Keeping with me the sense of His nearness
Remembering, too, the beauty there, and
His loving Kindness and Dearness.

Martha Keltto

Contentment is that bit of golden light
That touches hearts and makes them clearly shine,
That brings a new depth into human sight
And makes just simple things seem rich and fine.
It may be part of evening fireside talks
Or just a smile across a table length;
It may surround a woods on autumn walks
Or brighten faith with new-discovered strength.

Contentment is that ray that warms the soul
And gives new courage where it may be found;
It follows hearts across the farthest knoll,
And lucky is that heart where it abounds.
Contentment is a light that all may see
Whose source is found in great eternity.

Maxine McCray Miller

How precious is your constant love, O God;
All humanity takes refuge in the shadow of your wings.
Psalm 36:7 (TLB)

Today I climbed a mountain,
Every step I took with care;
And when I reached the summit,
I discovered God was there.

I heard Him in the rushing wind,
I saw Him in the sky,
I watched His artistry at work
As white clouds drifted by.

I felt His touch as sunbeams bright
Fell warm upon my face;
I gazed in wonder at His works,
Each in its proper place—

The trees, the grass, the lofty heights,
The rocks so rough and steep,
The summit of the hillside and
The valley dark and deep,

The shadows and the sunlight
Making patterns ever new.
Yes, all these wonders I could see
As I beheld the view!

My heart was filled with gratitude
As I was standing there;
The wealth of love within my soul
Made me a millionaire.

When trials and troubles seem to fall
Like raindrops from above,
Come with me to a mountaintop
And find anew God's love!

Esther Hirst

Jesus, Lover of My Soul

Charles Wesley
S.B. Marsh
1. Je - sus, Lov - er of my soul, Let me to Thy bos - om fly,
2. Oth - er ref - uge have I none; Hangs my help-less soul on Thee.
3. Thou, O Christ, art all I want; More than all in Thee I find.
4. Plen-teous grace with Thee is found, Grace to cov - er all my sin.
While the near - er wa - ters roll, While the tem - pest still is high!
Leave, ah, leave me not a - lone; Still sup-port and com - fort me!
Raise the fall - en, cheer the faint, Heal the sick, and lead the blind.
Let the heal - ing streams a-bound; Make and keep me pure with - in.
Hide me, O my Sav - iour, hide, Till the storm of life is past.
All my trust on Thee is stayed; All my help from Thee I bring.
Just and ho - ly is Thy name; I am all un - righ-teous-ness.
Thou of life the Foun-tain art; Free - ly let me take of Thee.
Safe in - to the ha - ven guide. Oh, re - ceive my soul at last!
Cov - er my de - fense-less head With the shad-ow of Thy wing.
False and full of sin I am; Thou art full of truth and grace.
Spring Thou up with - in my heart; Rise to all e - ter - ni - ty.

Love of God Casts Out Fear

Some weeks ago a snow-laden wind howled its way through our woods. The birches bent with its force; the Norways, stiffly upright, fought it proudly, although their branches quivered under the onslaught. Our conical suet feeder swung crazily, like a jerky gymnast showing off his tricks. To the side of the feeder, with his tiny claws dug deep into the suet, clung a chickadee, his black topped head bobbing as he hammered away at the chunk of fat. He was oblivious to the storm, oblivious to the wild ride the feeder was taking him on, oblivious to everything except his desire for food. Fear was no part of his thinking. Evidently birds have a built-in radar system that keeps them in touch with the Spirit within, hence, they know no fear.

A Bible verse we humans would do well to remember tells us that "God hath not given us the spirit of fear; but of power, and of love, and of a sound mind" (II Timothy 1:7). A corollary to that statement might be, "But there is a spirit in man: and the inspiration of the Almighty giveth them understanding" (Job 32:8). The time has come for us to recognize that Spirit within and be grateful for the understanding that comes through the inspiration of the Almighty. We need to understand that we need not fear. We need not fear war nor lack nor revolution nor economic disaster. We need not fear anything because God's gifts to us do not include fear. Fear is an unknown quantity in God's universe. John tells us that "perfect love casteth out fear" (I John 4:18). Love of whom? Love of God. Love of God casts out fear. How? Because we are assured "Thou wilt keep him in perfect peace, whose mind is stayed on thee" (Isaiah 26:3). If, then, in our love for Him we keep our minds stayed on God, we will be kept in perfect peace, and there can be no fear in peace that comes from the Father within.

Gertrude M. Puelicher

Not by Bread Alone

Kirby Page

Man does not live by bread alone, but by beauty and harmony, truth and goodness, work and play, affection and friendship, aspiration and worship.

Man does not live by bread alone, but by the splendor of the starry firmament at midnight, the glory of the heavens at dawn, the gorgeous blending of colors at sunset, the luxurious loveliness of magnolia trees, the sheer magnificence of mountains.

Man does not live by bread alone, but by the majesty of ocean breakers, the shimmer of moonlight on a calm lake, the flashing silver of a mountain torrent, the exquisite patterns of snow crystals, the exalted creations of master-artists.

Man does not live by bread alone, but by the sweet song of a mockingbird, the rustle of tall corn in the breeze, the magic of the maestro's violin, the sublimity of Beethoven's Fifth Symphony.

Man does not live by bread alone, but by the fragrance of roses, the scent of orange blossoms, the smell of new-mown hay, the clasp of a friend's hand, the tenderness of a mother's kiss.

Man does not live by bread alone, but by the lyrics and sonnets of poets, the mature wisdom of sages, the biographies of great souls, the life-giving works of Holy Scripture.

Man does not live by bread alone, but by comradeship and high adventure, seeking and finding, creating and cooperating, serving and sharing, loving and being loved.

For in Him we live and move and are!
Acts 17:28 (TLB)

There is so much I have not been,
so much I have not seen.
I have not thought and have not done
or felt enough—the early sun,
rain and the seasonal delight
of flocks of ducks and geese in flight,
the mysteries of late-at-night.

I still need time to read a book,
write poems, paint a picture, look
at scenes and faces dear to me.
There is something more to be
of value—something I should find
within myself—as peace of mind,
patience, grace and being kind.

I shall take and I shall give
while yet, there is so much to live
for—rainbows, stars that gleam,
the fields, the hills, the hope, the dream,
the truth that one must seek. I'll stay
here—treasure every day
and love the world in my own way!

Helen Harrington

The joy of life is living it and doing things of worth,
In making bright and fruitful all the barren spots of earth.

In facing odds and mastering them and rising from defeat,
And making true what once was false, and what was bitter, sweet.

For only he knows perfect joy whose little bit of soil
Is richer ground than what it was when he began to toil.

Author Unknown

What God
Hath Promised

God hath not promised
Skies always blue,
Flower-strewn pathways
All our lives through;
God hath not promised
Sun without rain,
Joy without sorrow,
Peace without pain.

But God hath promised
Strength for the day,
Rest for the labor,
Light for the way,
Grace for the trials,
Help from above,
Unfailing sympathy,
Undying love.

Annie Johnson Flint

Oh, to Live Beautifully

Oh, to live beautifully
For my brief hour
As does a wayside flower,
Unperturbed by the strange brevity
Of time allotted me;
Undisturbed by the overshadowing shine
Of tree and climbing vine;
Bravely stemming the wind and the beating rain,
Bowing and lifting again;
Within me some strong inner force as bright
As a poppy filled with light;
My feet firm-rooted in the earth's good sod,
My face turned toward God,
Yielding some fragrance down the paths I know
A little while . . . then go
As a flower goes, its petals seeking the ground
Without a cry or sound,
But leaving behind some gold seed lightly thinned
To blow upon the wind.

Grace Noll Crowell

God, keep within my soul
  a deep, cool well
Of living water, sweet and
  crystal clear,
Fresh as a sparkling spring
  within a dell,
So I may walk in gladness,
  not in fear.
For I am thirsty and would
  drink my fill...
Renew my strength from this
  life-giving stream
That soothes my restless mind,
  my stubborn will,
That brings to me the vision
  and the dream:
The dream of looking upward
  to the stars,
Of searching in their light
  that I may find
A way to break down all
  the prison bars,
The shackles and the fetters
  of the mind,
The dream of light where darkness dare not dwell.
God, keep within my soul
  a living well.

Frances Bowles

Lord, may my life be thus:
A perpetual incense lifting
  up to Thee.
As a flame lifts from a lamp
  at evening time,
Setting a clear light free,
So may the fragrance from some
  helpful word
That I may speak, lift skyward,
  and each deed
That blesses a worn traveler
  on his way
Be a sweet scent, indeed:
A perpetual incense, Lord,
Not that of one crushed flower
  beneath the feet,
But ever, always lifting
  up to Thee
A fragrance, clean and sweet,
From a life that is thy gracious
  gift to me.
I would not fail thee, Lord. Help
  me return
A lasting fragrance for thy gift,
  through this
Lit incense that I burn.

Grace Noll Crowell

Let me do good and never know
To whom my life a blessing brings;
Even as a lighthouse freely flings
O'er the dark waves a steady glow,
Guiding the ships which to and fro
Flirt by unseen with their
  white wings.
Let me do good and never know
To whom my life a blessing brings;
As thirsty travelers come and go
Where some fresh mossy
  fountain springs,
It cools their lips and
  sweetly sings,
And glides away with heedless flow.
Let me do good and never know
To whom my life a blessing brings.

Richard Wilton

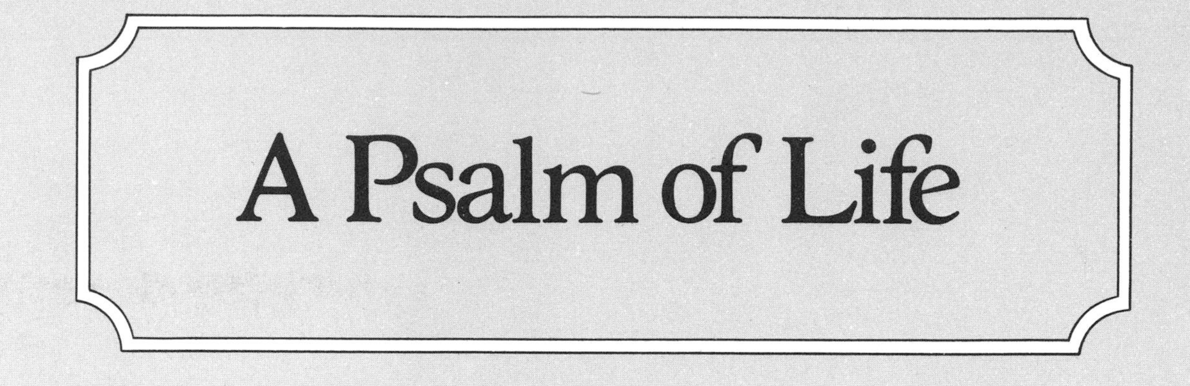

A Psalm of Life

Tell me not, in mournful numbers,
Life is but an empty dream!
For the soul is dead that slumbers,
And things are not what they seem.

Life is real! Life is earnest!
And the grave is not its goal;
Dust thou art, to dust returnest,
Was not spoken of the soul.

Not enjoyment, and not sorrow
Is our destined end or way;
But to act, that each tomorrow
Find us farther than today.

Art is long, and Time is fleeting,
And our hearts, though stout and brave,
Still, like muffled drums, are beating
Funeral marches to the grave.

In the world's broad field of battle,
In the bivouac of life,
Be not like dumb, driven cattle!
Be a hero in the strife!

Trust no Future, howe'er pleasant!
Let the dead Past bury its dead!
Act, act in the living Present!
Heart within, and God o'erhead!

Lives of great men all remind us
We can make our lives sublime,
And, departing, leave behind us
Footprints on the sand of time;

Footprints, that perhaps another,
Sailing o'er life's solemn main,
A forlorn and shipwrecked brother,
Seeing, shall take heart again.

Let us, then, be up and doing,
With a heart for any fate;
Still achieving, still pursuing,
Learn to labor and to wait.

Henry Wadsworth Longfellow